inking the world

inking the world

Don Gutteridge

First Edition

Hidden Brook Press
www.HiddenBrookPress.com
writers@HiddenBrookPress.com

Copyright © 2019 Hidden Brook Press
Copyright © 2019 Don Gutteridge

All rights for poems revert to the author. All rights for book, layout and design remain with Hidden Brook Press. No part of this book may be reproduced except by a reviewer who may quote brief passages in a review. The use of any part of this publication reproduced, transmitted in any form or by any means, electronic, mechanical, photocopied, recorded or otherwise stored in a retrieval system without prior written consent of the publisher is an infringement of the copyright law.

inking the world
by Don Gutteridge

Cover Design – Sol Terlson Kennedy
Layout and Design – Richard M. Grove

Typeset in Garamond
Printed and bound in Canada
Distributed in USA by Ingram, in Canada by Hidden Brook Distribution

Library and Archives Canada Cataloguing in Publication

Title: Inking the world / Don Gutteridge.
Names: Gutteridge, Don, 1937- author.
Description: First edition. | Poems.
Identifiers: Canadiana 20190079797 | ISBN 9781927725696 (softcover)
Classification: LCC PS8513.U85 I55 2019 | DDC C811/.54—dc23

Contents

– Inking the World – *p. 1*
– Vivid – *p. 2*
– Spin – *p. 3*
– Hum – *p. 4*
– Heft – *p. 5*
– Almost – *p. 6*
– Village – *p. 7*
– Rhymes – *p. 8*
– Such a Longing – *p. 9*
– Somebody Else – *p. 10*
– Speechless – *p. 11*
– Be – *p. 12*
– Forever – *p. 13*
– Universe – *p. 14*
– Tolling – *p. 15*
– Insurgent – *p. 16*
– Wide – *p. 17*
– Hopes – *p. 18*
– Roast – *p. 19*
– Alone – *p. 20*
– Luffed – *p. 21*
– Back Home – *p. 22*
– Small-Town Betrayal – *p. 24*
– Anguish – *p. 25*
– Tides – *p. 26*
– Starred – *p. 27*
– Zipper – *p. 28*
– Double – *p. 29*
– Wootser – *p. 30*
– Lifetime – *p. 31*

– Stretch – *p. 32*
– Heathen – *p. 33*
– Sundays – *p. 34*
– Being – *p. 35*
– Ruthless – *p. 36*
– There Was A Time – *p. 37*
– Joie De Vivre – *p. 38*
– Promise – *p. 39*
– Summer – *p. 40*
– Pop – *p. 41*
– Nimble – *p. 42*
– Such a Longing – *p. 43*
– Numinous – *p. 44*
– Luck – *p. 45*
– The Village Within – *p. 46*
– The Point of it All – *p. 1*
– Eternity – *p. 48*
– Stone's Throw – *p. 49*
– Bereft: A Suite – *p. 50*
– Bedizened – *p. 51*
– Bereft – *p. 52*
– Shakespearean – *p. 53*
– Long Sleep – *p. 54*
– Recalled – *p. 55*
– Syllables – *p. 56*
– All That's Said and Done – *p. 57*
– Perpetual – *p. 58*
– Shy – *p. 59*
– Linked – *p. 60*
– Patience – *p. 61*
– Au Revoir – *p. 62*
– Lifelong – *p. 63*

- Undaunted – *p. 64*
- Mutts – *p. 65*
- Embedded – *p. 66*
- Grateful – *p. 67*
- Otherwise – *p. 68*
- Gibbon's – *p. 69*
- Dixie – *p. 70*
- Anodyne – *p. 71*
- Proposal – *p. 72*
- Hesitation – *p. 73*
- Sacred – *p. 74*
- Hungering – *p. 75*
- Honeymoon Bay (2) – *p. 76*
- Absence – *p. 77*
- Bath – *p. 78*
- Whole – *p. 79*
- Pleasure – *p. 80*
- Anointed – *p. 81*
- Magic – *p. 82*
- Rhymed – *p. 83*
- For my Grandmother – *p. 84*
- Grief – *p. 85*
- Some Things – *p. 86*
- Music – *p. 87*
- Remembrance – *p. 88*
- Sweet Season – *p. 89*
- Forbidden – *p. 90*
- Dinner – *p. 91*
- Motive – *p. 92*
- Sweet Season – *p. 93*
- Charlie – *p. 94*
- Delight – *p. 95*

– Inked – *p. 96*
– Such An Urge – *p. 97*
– Soft and Low – *p. 98*
– Once Again – *p. 99*
– Tingle – *p. 100*
– Touch – *p. 101*
– Flaws – *p. 102*
– Walk – *p. 103*
– Saturday – *p. 104*
– Many a Night – *p. 105*
– Blessed – *p. 106*
– The Light – *p. 107*
– Beginning – *p. 108*
– Exegesis – *p. 109*
– Witting – *p. 110*
– Past – *p. 111*
– Village Dreaming – *p. 112*

About the Author – *p. 115*

Inking the World

Whenever I think of my demise
I try to remember the day
my mother, still a girl,
unwombed me and I swallowed
a village whole and kept it
tucked inside the little
room of my mind for eighty-
one years, and I have grown
gracefully old and somewhat
wiser, embracing my age
and inking the world with poems.

Vivid

When I delve more deeply
into the past, undaunted
by Time's treachery, I see
myself vivid in the village
that spawned me, a lad
of eleven, his head humming
with poems and stories about
to be born when the right
words begin their rhyming
and something magical
urges their birth, and I am
soon walking on the Heaven-
hewn stretch of Canatara's
sands under the sun's
strum, livid with light
and dreaming of endless authordom,
while the Earth still turns
on its steadfast axis.

Spin

If it wasn't Post Office
it was Spin the bottle:
anything to pin my lips
upon Shirley's cherub cheek
and watch her blush as the
rush of blood hit me
where I needed it most
and I thanked the Lord for the
gift of girls and the un-
throttling of male desire.

Hum

Shirley McCord was a drum
majorette in the Girl Guides
band, and she twirled her baton
with all the aplomb of a
Barnum-and-Bailey juggler,
and I watched her leading the parade
with a high-stepping, long-
legged stride, hugging
the pavement and making my heart
hum.

Heft

Wiz Withers, our guru
of gizmos and gadgets, was not
one to dawdle or dither:
he'd wave his magic wand
and presto! a go-kart
worthy of the Soap Box
Derby would pop up
fully functioning on the
Main Drag and we left
the cheering crowd in our dust,
speeding as quick as Herbie
Gilbert's flivver; another
wave and lo! the circus
we dazzled the denizens with
that summer of forty-seven,
and I was intoxicated with such
effortless wizardry and bowled
over by his being bigger
than I had ever imagined
myself to be, under
the heft of Heaven

Almost

When I was almost young
and lilacs hung on the hedge
that hugged us snugly in,
I never ventured beyond
our homestead's edge
or roamed into the indelible dark,
content to squeeze my panda
bear and watch Grandma's
Jello cooling on the verandah.

Village

There was a time when my village
seemed to me to be
paradisal, where the lilacs
grew more lavender
and the sun bloomed on its horizon
like a slow rose opening
to the lick of light, where friendships
were made as if forever
would never end, where the groomed
grass of grandfather's lawn
was as green as the leaves of Eden,
where home was the place that eased
us into the diligent dark,
and where the days were metrical
and all my poems rhymed.

Rhymes

Nancy Mara, I loved
you from afar: I was Lancelot
going for the Grail and I dreamed
you dulcet on Canatara's
singing sands and whenever
I closed my eyes I saw you
afloat on a star-brushed
horizon and I wanted to write
a dozen sonnets and dedicate
each one of them you:
scintillating with similes
and ringing with rhymes.

Such a Longing

I have such a longing
for the days that are no more,,
when the sun rose over
my boyhood town each
misted morning, hefting
light for my eyes only
as I circumnavigate the streets
(like LaSalle on the prowl
for gold and glory), looking
for the point poised between
the Lake and the River, greeting
each friend and rival
with equal ease, knowing
we shared this cozy
desmene, that ours was our own
story to tell, and that
we would never be bereft
of belonging.

Somebody Else

Strange what we remember
when old age creeps
alive into our capillaries:
the squeak of a rusted gate
when I strode out of my grandfather's
lot onto the welcoming
sidewalk and peddled my way
over granny-cracks
whose craqueleur I cannot
unforget, the squeal
of my trike's back wheel
and the heraldic honk of its horn,
startling Mister Robinson
and the banty rooster next
door, and thither I rode
past the immaculate lawn
of Bryant's groomed abode
(whose heart disassembled
from too much perfection),
and on by Gray's latticed
porch and the end of my designated
desmene: but try as we might,
nothing is born again,
the world withers away
without our saying until
we too are just somebody
else's memory.

Speechless

In my seething imagination
these dunes were here
when the last Neanderthal
stood upright on Canatara's
beach, blinking into the
morning sunlight
and pandering to clams fresh
from the Lake's cellarage
(an age before Adam
or Eden were dreamed), not
knowing he would soon be
extinct, that all things
flesh must pass away
speechless so other
beings, sir or madam,
can be born and Mother
Earth renewed in her glory
and an octogenarian poet
can stroll past these mesozoic
mounds and tell their story
in a birthing of words.

Be

I have such a longing
to see once again
the lush lavender of the lilacs
that hugged grandfather's lawn
and to feel one more time
the brush of a breeze combing
the leaves of our Manitoba maples
and to know the warmth of a home-
kitchen, love-tugged,
and to tingle with the touch of fingers
so tender I could dream
only of being in their embellished
embrace and I have such
a longing to be born again
in the place where I could merely
be.

Forever

When you reach four score
and a bit, your mind moves
to those scenes of your childhood
where you were free to roam
the fraternizing streets and greet
Wiz and Bones, Jerry
and Hutch and where the sun
solemnized the village that whittled
you into the world, and a lake
awaited your wading in its beryl-
blue waves and a breeze
dizzied the trees in Canatara
and where Nancy Mara had eyes
for you alone, and where home
was grandfather's lilac-
lit demesne and we all
thought ourselves clever
enough to make it last
forever.

Universe

I wake and the world widens,
and just beyond the morning
dews the Lake swims
into view like a slow fuse,
so blue it would blind Zeus
or make Oedipus blink,
and a breeze quickens to wimple
the waves swallowing each
other and licking the silence
of the shore, and I reach the water's
edge and immerse one
simple toe in Cameron's
granite chill, feel
the immanent will of the Universe,
inked and abiding.

Tolling

Ours was a three-steepled
town, when, on a Sunday
morning the tolling of deep-
tongued bells and their tuneful
music drew the people
of the Point to their pews and the
weekly anointment, free
for the moment of Sabbath sins
and the impious whims of Lucifer
and his less-than-holy crew.

Insurgent

The girls of my village sprawl
on the beaches of Canatara,
preening and prettifying in the
lilting light that prisms
off the Lake's face,
unaware that beauty
is its own grace, defying
all logic, all
reason, and these bodies,
embraced in biology, seasoned
by the noontide sun
and the sifting of silted sands,
leave the boys, beyond
reach on the nippled dunes,
un-willed, moon-
endued and prey to their most
insurgent urges.

Wide

Eleven and still unable
to swim, paddling in the Lake's
shallows like a inflated dolphin,
while Nancy and the girls
disport on an anchored raft
fifteen yards away
(all that flesh caressed
by the afternoon sun),
flashing me a smile
now and then before diving
slim-thighed into the nearest
breaker as slick as seals
into a tumescent sea, as the raft
tilts and sways like Noah's
craft on God's turbulent
tide, breasting the waves
and waving at one who
could not stroke his body
across a heavenly divide
that might has well have been
a mile wide.

Hopes

Shirley was the first girl
whose elongated legs caught
my amorous eye as she whirled
and danced at Double Dutch,
showing us once in a blue
menstrual moon a thimbleful
of thigh and what we imagined
lay higher up
between the taut squeeze
of her glorious gams, but Shirley
took no notice
of the male gaze for she
was skipping in frenzied bursts
to entertain and amaze,
until the ropes sagged
like spent balloons and she flashed
us a smile that said,
"I'm no bimbo,
but this may be romance,"
or such were our hopes.

Roast

Mrs. McCleister's cockerel
pulled the sun up
over the lip of the horizon
with his clawed beak and crowed
in the morning, his wattle waxing
as scarlet as a tanager, while
his hens feathered deeper
into their straw beds, wary
of his bottled fury, but the
widow next door didn't prize
his dawn song and threatened
to roast him for Easter.

Alone

My widowed grandmother
listening to the radio: soap
after soap carrying
from the dining room all
the way to the kitchen chair
where she sits knitting:
Helen Trent's romance
gives way to Pepper
Young's family – unless
the Tigers are playing at Briggs,
only then will she drop
a stitch or two with the crack
of the bat like wood on bone
or the thud of a pitch in the mitt
as the crowd cheers and she wishes
she could be anywhere
but here – unsung
and alone.

Luffed

How many hours did we spend
speculating what lay between
Shirley's girlish thighs,
caught as we were in the first
flush of lust's lustre,
our consensus (from a single glance
at her one-piece suit)
being a tuft that tingled
and tantalized or a petalled pucker
that fuelled our fancy and tested
our masculine mettle, but alas
remained taboo, taking
the wind out of our sails
and leaving us luffed?

Back Home
On a visit to the Point with my son
John on June 15, 2018

For what may well be
the last time, I re-see
the village that vaulted me
into being, unumbilicalled
into its flawless world
that is both estranging
and familiar, where some houses
have same gee-and-haw
tilt they had when I first
tricycled past them,
and there is grandfather's
mansion, where I re-imagine
the trees that lightning levelled
and the lilacs now beyond
blooming, and my son nods
when I point to the room
where I lay a-bed for seven
months and lived to tell
the story, and the Lake lives
again here and in my mind
in all its blue-belled
bevelled glory, and we stroll
by Mara's place, unchanged,
and bid goodbye to the empty
space where the streetlamp
supervised our glorious games
and the June moon summered
on the horizon like an angel's smile,

and we stare at Canatara
uplifted by light, and sit
for a while under the Bridge
and watch the steamers go
slowly by like a dream
of themselves and like
the flow of Time itself
and this gift given
by the gods only once.

Small-Town Betrayal

When our neighbor Mr. Hart
offered to buy my grandfather's
house with its half-acre
groomed grounds, Where I spend
my happiest childhood
days, he pleaded poverty
and appealed to my uncle, who made
him a deal: reduced price
for a vow not to sever
the lot, to keep its lilac
and foaming spirea hedges
as they were, and so
the sunny haven I thought of
as home passed to others,
and a year later Mr. Hart
severed the lot and made
a pot of money

Anguish

The languorous-limbed girls
of the Point languish on the sands
of Canatara in their one-
piece suits, and long
to be ogled by boys
with impish grins and hurled
hoots, while the mustard sun
anoints their new-blooming
bodies and Huron's wavelets
soothe the shameless shore
and nothing stirs in the
blush of the afternoon
but lust's unfulfillable
anguish.

Tides

It was the Ojibwa who gave us
"Canatara" for the "blue water"
of the big-bellied lake
that hugged the beach and its
mile-long stretch of
Saharan sand, a double
trochee rolling off
the aboriginal tongue
like the tunes of Orpheus, and I think
of those first peoples
offering a kind of birth
to those unbroken
sands and the cobalt swells
of a water-body wider
than half the seas on Earth
and mammoth enough to dwarf
their moon-tugged tides.

Starred

Under the moon's gossamer
glimmer, we go a-blading
on Leckie's iced-over
fallow, the wind-chill
raw against our cheeks
as hand-in-hand we scribble
scrimshaws into the shimmering
surface, traceries
of our having been, here
on this hallowed ground
on such a night, limned
by light, tremored by tingling
touch, and all beneath
the unmarred wonder
of the starred firmament.

Zipper

While the great Lake's
wavelets lick the shore
with lascivious lips, the girls
of the Point bask in the fiery
sun above Canatara, and do not
ask whether they are being statued
by the stare of boys who would do
a jig to see them au naturel
or put a zipper on their whirly-
gigging desires.

Double

Riding Double in the Point
was considered a sin akin
to eating apples in Eden,
but I was bike-free
and Butch's handle bar
beckoned, so we cycled
triumphantly through the hodge-podge
of alleys and lanes, dodging
Constable Pedan (hapless
on foot), untroubled
by doubt, certain we were a
force to be reckoned with,
and wishing Eve the best.

Wootser

Mrs. McCleister's blood-
wattled rooster serenaded
each sunrise
with his lascivious aria,
making the mottled hens
tremble with trepidation,
knowing that, feast or famine,
they would be boosted one
by one, and at last a triumphant
cry could be heard all
the way to Wooster, Mass.

Lifetime

My first story, cribbed
from the Grade Three primer,
garnered undeserved praise
from my teacher that not only
raised my spirits but made me
a believer, and so it was
no surprise two grades
later when I began filling
my scribblers with intrepid tales
of quibbling bears and duelling
rabbits with blinking blue
eyes, and finally my maiden
poem arrived, in rhyming
couplets, inked from a Muse
as demanding and she was un-
bribable, and soon the scribe
in me became habitual,
lasting a lifetime.

Stretch

If you don't mind cattails
like badly brushed hair
and the odd pair of pussy
willows encased in the ice
like butterflies from the
Pleistocene age jewelled
in amber, you might
find yourself sailing
alone across a stretch
of ready-made rink
with the wind cherubic on your cheeks,
fantasizing stanzas in snow
and sleek-paced poems
on a glazed page, etched
in indelible ink.

Heathen

"Don't worry," Butch
says as he dispatches
the adder with a hectic blow,
"Snakes always come
back to life again
at midnight." "The little
heathen," my Grandma says,
"What a concoction!"
When we hurry back
next day, the creature
lies in the grass, unalive.
"It's okay," Butch says,
"I don't believe in the
Resurrection either."

Sundays

On Sundays we sang of Jesus
and his glory and the precious blood
of the Lamb, our voices high,
as if we knew what it was
to be affixed to a cross
and have your highway
to Paradise paved,
or be strong enough to roll
that stone away and live
again – leaving us
to sing your story, and wonder.

Being

We come into this world
unbidden; there is
no-one to applaud
our irreverent arrival,
so we irrigate the air
with our prodigal cries,
succumb to the need
to breathe, somehow
inhabit the broad
acreage of that space
Nature grants us –
and celebrate the birth
of our being.

Ruthless

And me composing poems:
inklings I tease
towards some sense
in words whetted upon
the wheel of memory
and swerving askance
upon the page where they lean
upright, enlinked,
ready to be swallowed whole,
raw and ruthless
in rhythmic pursuit
of the truth.

There Was A Time

There was a time when I believed
that God inhabited the white
clapboard church
on Michigan Ave, seated
in the back pew, I could feel
His breath floating from the
sanctuary as light and healing
as a June breeze on my grand-
father's lilacs, I could hear
His unvoiced words and knew
that somewhere near
angels amplified the chancel
air, I said my rhyming
prayer each night before
I entered the slough of sleep,
begging the Lord to take
my soul if I should die
before waking, but oh
how relieved I was to see
the sun pouring through
my bedroom window
like a giddy doubter's dance:
yes, there was a time
when I believed, I really
did.

Joie De Vivre

We heard the Tin Lizzie
three blocks away, the ooga-
ooga horn blaring
abroad, as we rushed to the curb
to catch Herbie boogying
on by at full
throttle, with a grin on his face
that would have impressed the Wizard
of Oz, fedora flapping
and a wave and a wink at his fans
and our raucous applause,
before he wheeled homeward,
erased in a cloud of dizzying
dust: we loved the show
so much we wanted to bottle it.

Promise
For Isabelle Macdonald
In memoriam

In nineteen seventy-nine
I travelled the byroads
of Lambton County, armed
with a film and an audiotape:
attempting to prompt poems
out of budding Purdys,
and the at one school,
there at the back of the class-
room, squeezed into an under-
sized desk, sat
Miss Macdonald. my Grade
Three teacher, come
to see if I had fulfilled
the promise she'd drawn from me
with her partisan praise
of my ink-squibbed scribbles –
we smiled at each other
across a forty-year
divide, linked by a love
of words.

Summer
After John B Lee

What I remember most
are the sun-softened days
when we set out for the beach
like charlatan Champlains,
unhobbled by the heat,
out towels draped over
our fair-skinned shoulders
like cavalier's capes,
until we found the path
as familiar as our crease-streaked
palms and waved at the lighthouse
that stood alabaster and beckoning
at the edge of the wind-whetted
water, then welcomed the sands
of Canatara once again,
and let the waves flutter
over our unfettered feet
like tiny tongues licking
us lean, while we stood
stark in the free-flung
breeze, daring to be
the first to dive into the
cobalt, chilled undertow
and levitate like dolphins
flippered and flying through the
breakers, abetted by a north-
nudging wind, before exhaustion
claimed us and we flopped
like limp mops upon
the stinging, sun-stroked
sand, and wondered even then
how much of these doldrum.
summer-drifting days
we would always remember.

Pop
For My Grandfather

We called him "Pop"
because all the real
Dads were away at war,
we trailed behind his corporal's
stride, hopping from foot
to foot to keep pace,
as if he were the Pied Piper
and we his willing worshippers,
until we reached the work-
shop where he wrought wonders
with wood and delicately shorn
steel (we watched it peel
away from the oiled lathe
in tiny girlish curls),
thence to be rendered into whirl-y-
gigs the whole town prized,
and while he stood there
with his wide, patient smile,
we peppered him with our child's
questions about the world
and its doings, like Socrates
interrogating the Wise, and wished
the war would never end.

Nimble
For Rebecca and Katie

My granddaughters knitting,
sitting still as statues,
each stitch the itch
of a thought in the mind before
the fingers nimble it into
place: there is such serenity
in their faces as they re-imagine
this ages-old art
of women everywhere,
and carry it out
with loose-limbed grace

Such a Longing

I have such a longing
for the days that are no more,,
when the sun rose over
my boyhood town each
misted morning, hefting
light for my eyes only
as I circumnavigate the streets
(like LaSalle on the prowl
for gold and glory), looking
for the point poised between
the Lake and the River, greeting
each friend and rival
with equal ease, knowing
we shared this cozy
desmene, that ours was our own
story to tell, and that
we would never be bereft
of belonging.

Numinous

I shall not rage at the
dying of the light: I've lived
too long under a luminous
sun to be at odds
with death; my days have been deft
with delight with just enough
pain to keep me ept
and witting; I've filled a thousand
pages with my word-scattered
scrawl, but I have left
my legacy in the brightening
eyes of my children's children,
and when the time arrives,
I will go gentle into that
numinous night.

Luck

The Garden was so perfect
that Adam spent his days
plucking plums and pomegranates
(from trees rinsed
with rain and dried by sun)
and ogled the plump-thighed
creature he'd rib-delivered
(wondering what beauty was for),
while Eve eyed the apple
and prayed for something
lucky to happen.

The Village Within

We all have a village within,
a place where we go
when the world fails us,
the home-ground where every
face is familiar and child-
size, where the streets welcome
our walking and each house
is a variation of our own,
its idiosyncrasies known
and loved just for being
there from the beginning
when our eyes were as wide
as any horizon, when all
was new and unrehearsed:
O the tug of the town
that gave us birth is one
of the sweetest joys we know.

The Point of it All

The point of it all
was the village I was born to,
where each morning the sun
sizzled out of First Bush
on the eastern edge of everything
and eased me into its cushioned
arms, my pencil poised
to tell its stories, where village
characters startled the streets
with their Pickwickian ploys,
and I roamed the town with my pals
Butch, Bones and Wiz
in search of adventures I would weave
into plots-to-be, and where
the incandescent waters
(under a sky pricked
with stars) of Huron would engender
poem after poem, rhyme
after rhyme, where there was time
to savour the unjudged joy
of being among the anointed,
of making my point.

Eternity

O what a village
I was born to, where the
sun over First Bush
rises reinvented each
morning, layering its
lacquered light upon
streets fresh from a
hushed night's dreaming,
and I sally forth like a
sea-going Argonaut
for the ells and alleys where roses
grow umbilical on
barn-board fences,
ablaze in rhyming red,
and stiff-trunked trees
are surprised by breezes
breathing serenity, and I am
now Earth's original
cartographer, nosing
amongst the by-ways
and fractured shadow:
foraging for a future
unhorizoned by time
or eternity.

Stone's Throw

The creek that links Cameron
and Cyprus meanders along
like an adder sodden with sun
slinking through the reeds
and water-lilies floating
flamboyant on the mirrored
surface, and from whose pads
bullfrogs leap
on their tantalizing trapezes
and land with a punctuated plop
in shallows no deeper
than an elf's ankle, and so
it is that we have to pole
ourselves from bend
to bowing bend, soaking
in the morning's saffron glow
and savouring the soul of this
perfected place a stone's
throw from Eden.

Bereft: A Suite
For Anne in loving memory

Flower

If you were a flower, you'd be
a yellow rose, more rare
than pedestrian red or shrinking
pink: you would bloom on
your birthday every June
as faithfully as the moon
on her monthly quest about
the Earth, and I would build you
a bower where love mellows
the heart and affection flairs
and no-one has to die.

Bedizened

It began simply enough:
you asked me if I wished
to see an opera in T.O.,
and when I discovered what
that was, I agreed, and off
we went: two mates
on a big-town spree:
you the city sophisticate
with a roil of red hair
swept up like a nun's
wimple and sporting a lemon
dress a diva would die for,
me the country tyro, just
glad to be along
for the ride, and after Tosca
and Lois at the Massey,
when your blue eyes made
the moon glow golden,
and after the bliss of our first
kiss, surprising us both,
romance reared its bedizened
head, and from that time
on we danced as a duo.

Bereft

A pair of mated robins.
their bobbing throats a-throb
with parental song, gather
twigs and stray leaves
to build a nest along
our flowering trellis, feathered
and egg-ready: there's
going to be trouble you say
as day after day the birds
double their efforts to feed
the newborn chicks
with their stretched necks
and jerking jaws, but sure
enough there is a hitch
in the wind and the nest teeters
undeftly to the ground
where the young perish alone,
and I wonder if the parents
mourn their loss as humans
do when a quirk in the world's
weather leaves us bereft.

Shakespearean
For Anne in loving memory

We weren't exactly Romeo
and Juliet in their exuberant youth
and first single of touch,
nor Antony and Cleopatra leavened
by lust: there was nothing
Shakespearean about our love
or its five-act iambics,
we just enjoyed one
another's company, found
our singular souls compatible,
built ourselves a jewelled
home, persevered through laughter
and tears, and carried on
for fifty-seven years.

Long Sleep

Sometimes I wish
there really was a Heaven
and a grandfatherly God
to hold you in His arms
and bring you comfort in your long
sleep, but most of the time
I realize the soul is what
the eyes give in the here
and now, and that you left
us the second your lids
shut out your last room
and me, and the soul is also
whatever lingers
of you in the air I breathe
and the memories we made
together in mutual delight,
when my world still turned
and my heart was leavened
with light.

Recalled

I am reminded that you
are gone every time
I look at your photo on the
Free Press obit,
whose framed face smiles
down at me, and while
I can dream you alive,
I cannot fill the empty
rooms you graced with your perpetual
presence or erase the memories
that soothe and scald, coming
in waves that overwhelm,
and oh how I wish I could see
you sit in your favourite place
just once more,
reach out, touch you
and talk of a charmed life
recalled.

Syllables

I've often thought, penning
a verse, that it could be
my last, the inner voice
I've both blessed and cursed
for more than sixty years
muffled forever, but such
a loss would be nothing to your
leaving us: all the words
you used to lavish love,
kindle your million kindnesses
and make our house a home –
abruptly ended, but to me
you are worth above the thousand
poems I now send to you
in the syllables of your silence.

All That's Said and Done

The verses I scribble do not
change the world or move
the Earth tilting on its axis,
but nonetheless I carry on
as if my stilted stanzas,
coming as they do in dribs
and drabs, really counted:
for what else embodies
our longing for affection, our cry
at the demise of the light, our quarrels
with a fractious God, or the grief
I feel at losing you, scattered
across these raging
pages, where I find consolation
in the willingness of words,
knowing that, when all
is said and done, you were
the only poem that mattered?

Perpetual

My grief is a peripatetic pendulum
that swings from hard-
won resignation to sudden
bursts of tears that come
unbidden as I contemplate
the years I will have to live
without your love singing
to my soul, comforting
and ending these throbbing
sobs, while your fingers
brush my brow and sweep
the pain away, and your voice
reassures me of a perpetual
presence poised and ready
to reignite our love
and its fiery fiefdom.

Shy

You were always shy of the camera,
and whenever its intruding eye
took dead aim,
you hugged the nearest child
as a shield to share your smile
and let us know you were exuding
love, not a photo yielding
nothing but tugs of vanity,
and so, when we were searching
for a snapshot to grace
your obit, we had to crop
a family view, and, heart-
heavy, I sit staring
at it across this room,
even as I imagine you,
ever true to your own
tune, wince at my grieving
glance, amused at the world's
inanities.

Linked

For fifty-seven years
we occupied the same space,
sometimes rooms
apart, other times
side by side on the
chesterfield, where we cozied
in coupled harmony, the yellow
roses you so prized
winking from the window-sill:
you who were never thrifty
with your affection, me
your willing paramour,
and as we aged gracefully,
our lives, enlinked more
and more, were groomed with a bliss
the Heavens would envy: now
you are gone and I am left
with nothing to say except
I miss you.

Patience

Patience was your password:
a hurting child, lad
or lass, in your arms was soon
soothed, embodied with love,
you waited out the minutes
while one of your pupils stuttered
over a letter until she got it
upright, and you smoothed
brows till the tears un-
uttered themselves
and your smile charmed them
into lilting laughter, and like Orpheus
the moving music of your voice
could tame the wildest canine
and make its tail wag
in grateful delight, but most
of all you suffered the way-
ward ways of the world
and tolerated God's oddities.

Au Revoir

I do not empty this house
of your presence: you are here
in every room we shared
breath in, your clothes still
hang where they belong
in their closets, and every painting
that adorns our walls is a reminder
of your artist's eye, and the chesterfield,
your bête noir, still
bears your imprint, and a novel
lies where your fingers last
lingered, nor am I made
forlorn on entering the space
now vacant of the woman
I cossetted and cradled with
love in its essence, for we are taught
that death is not an ending,
not goodbye but au revoir:
I refuse that platitude,
preferring your haunting hover
and the remnants of the things you touched
with such tenderness.

Lifelong

It will take me some time
to forget your final glance
as you lay rigoured by death
in your slack-jawed, breathless
body, your lids mercifully
closed, but I will try
by choosing to remember the freckle-
flecked, blue-eyed
beauty I first observed
across a schoolroom,
and saw that face again
each sun-burst
morning of our lifelong,
grace-bedewed romance.

Undaunted

Our biweekly jaunts
to the big city did not go
unremarked by our town-
folks: tongues wagged
when we whirled up in front
of my boarding house in your brand-
new Volks like lovers
unafraid of their affair,
we shocked the gentry, as window
blinds sagged discreetly
and we essayed a chaste kiss
in the cheerful dark of the car,
but I wanted the world to know
I had found a girl with copper
locks who kissed me back,
who cared nothing for what
the locals deemed proper,
and we carried on undaunted
for fifty-seven years.

Mutts

You led a dog's life,
surrounded by hounds, Scotties,
malamutes, pugs
and other ilk, they walked
you daily (one by one
or in twos and threes) through
Gibbon's Park, that manicured
meadow of silken grasses
and willowing trees, where
mistress and mutt could commune
in peace, for you spoke the lingo
of dogdom, and the love
they brought you was returned
ten-fold, singing
into their canine hearts,
with a little left over
for me.

Embedded

It wasn't a fancy wedding,
a party of six including
the bride and groom in the county
courthouse with a courtly
judge who slipped me a lucky
dime to dance on for a lifetime,
but you lit up the room like a
bloom-burst of stars
in a night sky, the radiance
of your face leaving me breathless,
transfixed by your beauty,
and with thoughts of the romance
we confected, each of us
exuding joy at the other's delight,
our love abiding, embedded
with affection.

Grateful

I was too shy to say
hello to you, so you
kindly said it for me,
and while it occurred to me
to ask for a date, I was
nonplussed by your smart
dress and sporty Volks
and that sophisticated up-
sweep of copper hair,
with eyes as blue as a heron's
April wing or the sky
when morning breaks upon
the world, but to no-one's
surprise you smiled me
supine and I offered you
my grateful heart.

Otherwise

In your last days you drew
into yourself, as if you knew
what was to come, you who
loved people and parties
at New Year's or any
time the spirit moved,
where we danced until the moon
abandoned its skies: you
with a smile as wide as the
lake we both adored,
and, ever outgoing, you made
fast friends that lingered
lifelong, and I watched
your slow descent with a stricken
heart, unwilling, though you
thought otherwise, to let
you go.

Gibbon's

Oh how you loved Gibbon's,
the park where willows wept
elongated tears and grasses
swooned like wind whirring
through wheat, where dogs loped
leash-free and owls
with their cowled frowns
found treetops
to their liking, where you made
lifelong friends
and stroked their canine companions,
a meadow you loved more than
Eve loved Eden when she popped
out of Adam's rib.

Dixie

This sumac, your favourite
tree, looms over our yard
and, once bristling with birds
and teetering with squirrels, is now
in its last throes, like all
those things we love
going in their good time,
and O how tickled
you were at a chickadee's
flickering flair, a cardinal's
scarlet calisthenics,
a robin's bashful bobbing,
and when I saw you in the hilt
of your happiness, I wanted to shout
Hallelujah or whistle
Dixie.

Anodyne

I weep because tears are an
anodyne against the grief
that consumes me at odd
times of the day and night,
it rises up unannounced
and overwhelms as I think
of all the years your face
was the first thing I saw
wakening each memorable
morning, and your eyes unfurling
blue upon our shared
world, and I think of those
days when we were blessed
with the benediction of our bodies
and our belief in the gratuity of grace,
but most of all I weep
because somewhere
some malign god
has forsaken me.

Proposal

It wasn't an elegant proposal
out of some fiery paperback
romance as we sat in your Volks-
mobile with the February snow
brushing the windshield
with feathered wispings, but you
said yes anyway, provided
there would be no bridal
showers, fancy engagement ring
or a fifty-plate wedding
supper, and I knew then
that you were your own woman
who knew life was no
bed of roses and would not
be rushed whatever the weather
or the stridency of my desire

Hesitation

Our home is exactly as it was
when your heart hesitated for the
last time: your clothes
hang in your closets ready
to be worn should you decide
to return, your coffee cup
awaits your nightly sip:
I cannot bear to part
with them any more than I can
bear the thought of losing you
as I roam from room to empty
room, stopping always
at the urn where you are resident,
relaxed in your final plot,
while the world and I continue
on our frantic axes, as doomed
as the yellow roses (you loved)
starved of slow light.

Sacred

Whenever I think of you in the
deep doldrums of my elongated
nights, I see Eve
in the glory of that dappled garden,
steeped in sunlight
that never unshone,
her naïve nudity haloed
to shape the suggestion of breasts
and the shadow where thigh
joins thigh, and set her locks
aglow like a nun's wimple,
and I think of that moment
when Adam first spied
his rib-ripped mate
and the blast that sight
must have made and eased
her story of an adder and an apple
into the conscience of his loins,
for beauty, like yours and hers,
with its simple sensuosity
hums in the heart and makes
remembering something
both aching and sacred.

Hungering

Each night since you've gone
I dream you alive: you are
a younger reflection of yourself:
your eyes as blue as flax
in bloom, your hair flowing
like cinnamon through my fingers
with a smile that says to the world:
I am thriving and together
we will dabble our days in delight,
O how wonderful
it is just to let our bodies
be, afloat in the Lake
of possibility, to take excursions
into felicity, babble our joint
joys and pray not to wake
as I now do, while the room
leaves me hungering after
any version of you.

Honeymoon Bay (2)

I still remember that evening
we spent on Honeymoon Bay,
lacquered with starlight
and waves shallowing the shore
like my fingers lovingly through
your lingering locks and a
breeze that crooned to the
evergreens cupping
our little encampment,
and we watched the Night come
slowly down like a lover's
lids, and to no-one's surprise
our bodies met, mused
serene, and fraternized.

Absence

Absence cannot be touched
or tasted: it lies in the
desmene of feeling when we yearn
for what cannot be,
it is the hollow where your head
lay, the room no one
like you occupies: I feel
its perpetual presence as the days
go on and on, I feel
it in the morning when I turn
and you are gone.

Bath

O how you loved your daily
soak, the tub filled
to the brim with boiling hot
water, suds-sudden,
into which you slowly submerged
like a lithe submarine, your flesh
afloat, weightless, tingling
in the sea-soft surround,
as if it were revisiting
the mother-womb that held
us bobbing in its warm amniotic
welcome: ands so during
your last days when you couldn't
make it up the stairs,
I knew I was going to lose you,
and never gain would I hear
a bath running without
a throb in the throat.

Whole

They say weeping is good
for the soul, but I find no
solace in the sobs that wrack
my body alive, and like
a man with an amputated limb,
I still believe the appendage
is there and thriving: I do not
wish to live amongst your memories,
as sweet as they may be:
I want you here – and whole.

Pleasure

What pleasure I took in exploring
the boundaries of your beautiful
body, the tingling of touch,
the trepidation of lip on lip,
my face reflecting yours,
the sigh of thigh against thigh,
for it is in the meshing of flesh
that our souls sing to one
another, my breath breathing
the ept essence of your own,
our separate selves longing
to be, for the measure of a minute,
a single being, knowing
in our hearts that we all
are destined to live apart,
as I do, with your graceful
going.

Anointed

Easter Sunday in the Point
was new shoes with the shine
still on them and pants
with a fine crease and ladies
bonneted and beribboned
and gentlemen in fresh habits,
and I remember staring at Christ
strung upon Golgotha (vinegar-
tongued, palms pinned
like moths on a lepidopterist's
display) just above
the altar where the Sabbath sun
limned His halo, and we felt
ourselves to be among
the anointed there, buoyed
by the yeast of prayer.

Magic

Cameron Lake is a pellucid
blue, and Tom and I
cavort in its chill welcome
like tantalizing tortoises:
now lolling on our plastic
mattresses, now diving
like deft dolphins or orphaned
Orcas, and when we've had
our fill, we lie upon
the sun-saturated sand
and let the wind dry
us benign, certain
that this magical moment
will be everlasting.

Rhymed

This photograph
of my grandsons cavorting
in the front seat of my Ford
Tempo (as green as grass
garnished with rain) is a
frozen moment I cherish:
James looks as if he's about
to seize the wheel and mosey
off like an importunate imp,
and Tim's baffled grin
at this peevish possibility
leaves me laughing, and grateful
that some things beyond
the instigations of Time
can come to pass un-
varnished and perfectly rhymed.

For my Grandmother

When grandfather died
your world was abruptly halved,
all those little rituals
that bound you one to one
now ended, you could not bear
ever again to sleep
in the bed you shared for more
than fifty years, your dreams
entangled through the long night
until morning woke you
with a new day, I remember
you best in the evenings,
you knitting in the kitchen,
Gramps snoozing through the news
a room away, but both of you
linked by love.

Grief

The night I first heard
my father cry: a single
anguished utterance,
the Earth tilted on its axis
half an inch or more,
and I thought of the oak
sturdy in our yard bent to
breaking in a tormenting wind,
and everything I'd known
and trusted was suddenly
as fragile as the life
of my dying grandfather,
and grief was a live being
with little time for childish
tears.

Some Things

At precisely ten after six
every Saturday evening,
just past closing
time at the Balmoral,
Bob McCord staggered
past our house, singing
off-key and entertaining
the street all along his way-
ward route; we'd watch
him enter his front door
and stumble into silence,
after which came the slap
heard round the village.
And sometime later
Mrs. McCord would appear
on her front porch as if
nothing had happened,
smiling grimly at those
unashamed enough
to pass by, and young
though I was, I thought:
this is the way things are
in our town, and then:
there are some things
that shouldn't be.

Music

On Good Friday we sang
of Jesus and His Precious Blood,
dripping from His hob-nailed
hands and feet on that
grim Golgotha, and dreamt
of an Easter morning when the sun
rose and solemnized
an empty tomb with the
stone rolled wondrously
away, and we felt a new
music throb in our throats.

Remembrance
For My Grandfather
In Loving Memory

Did you hear the sonorous
soaring of the Last Post
over your country's memorial,
the bugle singing as sadly
sweet as Gabriel's music
commemorating the brave in their
quiet graves, or the roaring
of the jets in salubrious salute?
Did you, my gloried grandfather,
come awake at such
concatenation, recall
your days doleful in that
far-away war?
No longer feel forsaken
by the souls you fought so
valiantly to save? Be
assured, we will remember,
though Time itself flies,
until the Earth un-
endures and the sun dies.

Sweet Season
For Anne in loving memory

When love bloomed in the sweet
season of lilacs and lilies,
we clung to each other
with such fierce felicity
that we wondered if love
could last and how the years
would treat the tendrill'd touch
of our embering affection, but then
you pierced my hectic heart
with your gifted glance, and we faced
the future free of fears,
remembering still the time
when lilacs bloomed like the
ungroomed gardens of Eden.

Forbidden

Whatever was forbidden
drew us towards it
like moths to a mammoth moon:
we were warned against The Slip,
too deep for dog-
paddling neophytes,
or hoboes with their anguished
eyes, or the Pool Room,
where we were addled by the
slick click of cue
on ball and the thwack of the
struck pocket (hidden
strictly from view), and we
wondered what shenanigans
our parents got up to
when the blinds came down,
or what strange terrain
was squeezed between the thighs
of girls we worshipped
from afar, too shy
to say hello or goodbye,
we rode our bikes double
to tease Pedan, our slew-
footed cop, and most
of all we dared the indelible
dark that each evening
enveiled our village –
a long ways East
of Eden.

Dinner

Mrs. McCleister's rooster
serenaded our street the moment
the morning sun tickled
his wattle, and then paraded
among his hens, crowing
over every conquest,
loud enough to make
a village wince, and boost
his gallic ego, till
my grandmother, losing
her legendary patience,
threatened to throttle him
and make him the principal
guest at her Easter dinner.

Motive
Point Edward: 1948

The village that spawned me
and kept me cozy
for a dozen years, was pointless
(I searched for it one
day and came home
puzzled) and long ago
was a railway town
bustling with locomotives
and a switching yard, until,
like railroads everywhere,
they pulled up the tracks
and skedadelled, leaving
a single line to rust
away (and a village shrunken,
out-of-joint with the world),
a set of tracks we trod
our on way to Canatara
where the faithful
Lake was motive enough
for a day's play (while
the sun-nuzzled dunes
warmed us, where we clambered
on amber afternoons)
and the slow walk home
along those ties
where we felt the heft of history
and realized the point of it all.

Sweet Season
For Anne in loving memory

When love bloomed in the sweet
season of lilacs and lilies,
we clung to each other
with such fierce felicity
that we wondered if love
could last and how the years
would treat the tendrill'd touch
of our embering affection, but then
you pierced my hectic heart
with your gifted glance, and we faced
the future free of fears,
remembering still the time
when lilacs bloomed like the
ungroomed gardens of Eden.

Charlie

Charlie was our neighbour,
a decorated vet who weathered
his nightmares with whiskey,
and, when that wouldn't do,
in beer binges at the Balmoral,
but nothing could unhinge
his image-riddled mind,
not even his three beautiful
daughters who doted on him
and us, and pretended not
to see that smile with the ache
in the middle.

Delight

When it was hide-and-go-seek
the girls of my village played
with all the pizzazz of Amazonians,
venturing into the virgin dark
beyond the umbrella-ed spray
of Mara's lamp to find
a cozy coign where many
a male purloined the swell
of a mislaid ankle
or a leg uncurling in the
shadows shredded by Mara's
light and at the All-Free
boys and girls together
emerged, outrunning
their breath, as if nothing
momentous had happened,
as if our un-Presbyterian
urges were our everyday
delight.

Inked

Nothing could dampen our spirits
under Mara's lamp,
not the monsoon moon or the
stark startling of stars
in the dark of a brooding sky,
and always it was hide-
and-go-seek when we out-
ran our own shadows
along Monk Street all
the way to the village brink
where we conversed with the universe,
for we were young and free,
inked with innocence.

Such An Urge

It might have been the moon-
light lacquering the black
length of Monk Street
or perhaps Mara's lamp
shrivelling the shadow around it,
but something in the air
that night drew us to the
farthest dark where an errant
knee might be harvested
by fingers a-tremble with touch,
or lips on lingering lips
in the grip of some desire
so fleeting we wondered
if such an urge could ever
be.

Soft and Low
For Anne in loving memory
and after The Bard and Dylan Thomas

Like Cordelia's, your voice
was ever soft and low,
a lovely thing in woman,
and like Lear I could cradle
you in my aching arms and
shed a tear or howl
my grief to Heaven aloft,
for your sudden going has left me
bereft of all but the memory
of our iambic dance and a plighted
troth that budded and bloomed,
epic in owl-light.

Once Again
For Anne in loving memory

Once again I stare
at our wedding photo (black-
and-white: we couldn't afford
colour), the only record
of our joyous nuptials, the two
of us on tip-toes
on brother-in-law's lawn,
nose to nose, our smiles
commingling, as if the future
lay before us, un-
ruptured, and I longed to swallow
you whole, grateful for the gift
of your self-effacing grace,
and knowing that you would always
sing to my soul.

Tingle
For Anne in loving memory

I cannot hug a memory
or squeeze the image of you
detonating in my dreams,
for we are made of blood
and bitter bone, and need
the feel of flesh enmeshed,
lips ellipsing lips
and skin skittering on skin,
and so it is we are not meant
to be alone without
the singular tingle of love's
hug.

Touch
For Anne in loving memory

There was a time when we simply
let our bodies be, and found
solace in the other's touch,
(as tangled as a rhyming couplet)
and I let my fingers scroll
through your tangerine tresses
with such tenderness that my breath
abandons, and I know the feel
of you whole, hearken to
your lean heartbeat
and say "God bless"
to the dimpled dark.

Flaws
For Anne in loving memory

I loved you because you were always
yourself and not an appendage
to my ego; I loved you because
you took my name and gave it
to our children to cherish; I loved
you because you made me feel
as if I could be whatever
the world offered; I loved you
because, above all,
you loved me, and now
that you are gone, I can love
the memories we made and let them
live on.

Walk

Every Sunday morning
my grandfather exercised
his heart, weakened by three
years in Belgium's maelstrom,
and me quick-stepping
a pace behind his corporal's
stride, firing questions
at him with Socratic aplomb
and waiting for his wise replies,
marvelling at his graceful patience
as we wended our way around
the home village — a thousand
miles from the horrific hum
of Howitzers.

Saturday

Grandfather in his Saturday
morning workshop,
and me barely seven,
watching his steadfast fingers
soothing the lathe or nudging
a lozenge of oak through the
stutter of the bandsaw,
and I felt blessed to be
born to such moments,
to be enhoused by love,
to be utterly endeared
as I waited for his hand
to drift down and tousle
my hair.

Many a Night
For Anne in loving memory

Many a night I dream
you alive once again
and O how I want you to be
so much more than
a memory, for I need to feel
the warmth of your beguiling
 smile upon the cheeks
you cherished and know the dance
of delight in your Baltic blue
eyes and run my fingers
through the rippling rust of your hair,
as I strive to live without the loving
lustre of your glance.

Blessed
For Anne in loving memory

Does anybody know how deep
love goes or how radiant
a rose can be in the luminous
light of a June morning,
for we are born to love
and beauty, despite the odds,
and we suffer heartbreak
and loss like heroic stoics,
and I have known it all
since you first flowed
into view and we fashioned a life
together, blessed by fortune,
embossed by the gods, passionate
and true.

The Light

I say goodnight to the
abstemious dark and drift
down to the dream-world
just below sleep,
whose images lift free
from their ordinary moorings
like prose poems without
rhyme or reason, dyed
deep with meaning beyond
the reach of mind or matter
which I may yet employ
in the daytime business
of iambicising, while I wait
for the chatter of robins saluting
the sun as it solemnizes the light.

Beginning
For Anne in loving memory

You were always your own woman:
I watched in awe, on those
days we fraternized in T.O.,
your cinnamon locks up-
swept in high style,
your lemon frock clinging
to every bow and curve,
your eyes ablaze with the vim
of a girl who promenaded
with pride through the Big City
beside a country bumpkin
like me, her smile dazzling
the denizens we passed on our way
to a beautiful beginning.

Exegesis
After Robert Browning

Approaching a poem should be
an act of love where one
soul opens itself
to another's textual touch,
where words are tasted on the tongue
and syllables sing us whole
again and tropes open
the heart to hope and similes
simulate in symmetries, where language
leaps alive with unredacted
truth and script is holier
than Scripture and exegesis
is ecstasy.

Witting

With what witting wonder
did my ten-year-old
eyes watch my father's
every move? Mixing
concrete, its lime seasoned
with sand and a soupçon
of liquid, stroking back
and forth like a lover's caress
or a minstrel's metronome
and then his trowel pasting
the stew-rich mass
onto cinder blocks
he nudged into place row
by row, judging the precise
line with a taut string
that pinged against the perpendicular
and I thought I knew this man
and the things he could do
with his hands, making me
a house I would soon call
home, the struts of its roof
angled against the symmetries
of the sun's leavening light
like raw-boned ribs
and the beads of my father's sweat
bedewed his brow and garnished
that all-embracing smile
and I felt as Elijah felt
at Heaven's gate.

Past

What I remember most
is the lake of grandfather's
lawn and lilacs lecherous
with light and bees inhabiting
the hollyhocks my grandmother
grew on the barnboard
fence and the lush pose
of the labyrinthine rose,
and I spent my days jousting
with joy and knew even
then that nothing lasts,
that what is present is already
past.

Village Dreaming

Rocking in my chair I dream
of the village where I was breathed
into being by the athletic lusts
of my hockey-heroing father
and the girl he deemed his paramour,
when my world was as new as a
chick picking at the shell
and a blank page I wrote
myself upon with words
wrestled from the womb, and a town
surrounded me with folks
to people my poems and startle
the stories I would create, in the
mortar and pestle of my imagination,
of their forgivable follies, the hustle
and bustle of their Dickensian lives,
and those childhood
chums I turned into combed
prose, who made my days
worth the telling and strummed
the strings of my memory, leaving
me to dream, rock and sing
the song of myself.

Don Gutteridge was born in Sarnia and raised in the nearby village of Point Edward. He taught High School English for seven years, later becoming a Professor in the Faculty of Education at Western University, where he is now Professor Emeritus. He is the author of seventy books: poetry, fiction and scholarly works in educational theory and practice. He has published twenty-two novels, including the twelve-volume Marc Edwards mystery series, and thirty-two books of poetry, one of which, *Coppermine*, was short-listed for the 1973 Governor-General's Award. In 1970 he won the UWO President's Medal for the best periodical poem of that year, "Death At Quebec." To listen to interviews with the author, go to: http://thereandthen.podbean.com. Don lives in London, Ontario.

www.ingramcontent.com/pod-product-compliance
Lightning Source LLC
Chambersburg PA
CBHW030120100526
44591CB00009B/476